ZODIAC

GTR MANCHESTER VOL II

Edited by Lucy Jeacock

First published in Great Britain in 2002 by
YOUNG WRITERS
Remus House,
Coltsfoot Drive,
Peterborough, PE2 9JX
Telephone (01733) 890066

HB ISBN 0 75433 648 4
SB ISBN 0 75433 649 2

FOREWORD

Young Writers was established in 1991 with the aim of promoting creative writing in children, to make reading and writing poetry fun.

Once again, this year proved to be a tremendous success with over 41,000 entries received nationwide.

The Zodiac competition has shown us the high standard of work and effort that children are capable of today. The competition has given us a vivid insight into the thoughts and experiences of today's younger generation. It is a reflection of the enthusiasm and creativity that teachers have injected into their pupils, and it shines clearly within this anthology.

The task of selecting poems was a difficult one, but nevertheless, an enjoyable experience. We hope you are as pleased with the final selection in *Zodiac Gtr Manchester Vol II* as we are.

CONTENTS

The Swinton High School

Trinity CE High School

Wright Robinson Sports College

The Poems

WATER

Fast, vicious and vain
Water can be compared to
A rapid storm of lightning,
On its way to the sea,
It is provoking contests,
Against all things tall and small,
Waves are frantically rising high,
So high they perform an act,
An act which equals flood,
The flood so sudden,
That the journey is almost complete,
An unexpected flash
And the river entwines the sea.

Melissa Zvinoira

THE ANNOYING BEAR

I wake up every morning
With a frightening scare
By the sound of a snoring
From a huge, fluffy bear.
When I tell him to stop he doesn't care
And sometimes he gives me a big nightmare.

At breakfast, he sits on two chairs,
I look at him and he stares.
He pulls the plate very slightly
Without asking for it politely,
And opens his eyes brightly.

At work, he plays with my private phones
He puts on all my favourite tones.
'Will you stop it?' I scream out
Until all my friends hear my loud shout.
He breaks the statue of the bumblebee
And spills my biscuits and my tea!

At lunch, he had a nasty dish
With mud, slugs and rotten fish!
He chewed through it like a chocolate eclair,
And pretended he didn't really care.
A fella like him you'd like to ignore,
No matter if you were rich or even poor.

Elham Ibrahem (12)
Abraham Moss High School

IN THIS WORLD, WE WILL NEVER MEET

In this world, we will never meet
Because if we do, we will then have to go into Hell's heat,
So therefore R . . . I'm stating to you clearly
That I love you so much and so dearly.
But only in Heaven, we will be together,
Where I will tell God, how much I loved you
And wanted you forever,
Then maybe in God's presence,
I will tell you face to face,
How lonely I lived without you,
In this world, with a gap in my heart . . .
. . . which was your space.

Asia Suleman (14)
Abraham Moss High School

WITHOUT FAREWELL

Without farewell
You fell asleep
For us and everyone to keep . . .
Gone are the happy days of the past
But wonderful memories
That will not die but last.
We all hope you are in peace
And looking down and watching us
At least . . .

Zile Huma (14)
Abraham Moss High School

MEMORIES

Gates of memories will never close
How much I miss you no one knows
Tears in my eyes will wipe away
But the pain in my heart will always stay.

Mariam Baloch (15)
Abraham Moss High School

A Rabbit Runs Very Fast

A rabbit runs very fast
A slow turtle comes always last
Wet rain drops from the sky
A red umbrella keeps me always dry
A fat hippo big and round
A thin snake on the ground
Inside my home it's dry and warm
Outside it is raining. What a storm!
I chased my ball during the day
At night I sleep, too tired to play
An empty bowl with nothing in
Now it is full right to the rim,
Balloons flat, light and free
A suitcase heavy as can be
A tall giraffe does not see
Someone who is short like me.

Besir Rysha (12)
Abraham Moss High School

MARTIN LUTHER KING

He always wanted everyone to live in peace,
With no wars on innocent countries being seized,
He wanted to spread harmony and love,
But a cruel person killed him and
Sent him up above . . .

Mariyam Suleman (12)
Abraham Moss High School

A RECIPE TO RECOVER DISASTER

Get two presidents who work in peace and harmony,
Drizzle into a bowl,
Mix in a load of friendship,
Whisk in a million ounces of care,
Season in some people who are willing to work together,
Add a big lump of love,
A large amount of laughter would throw away the tears
Place in some happy endings to flavour,
Spill out the bad senses which seem to despair
Bring in all the happiness which seems to have been thrown away,
Throw away all the greed and hatred,
Bring in all the love and care,
Stir in all the thoughtfulness and knowledge,
Separate racism and tolerance,
Batter well and throw away,
Discover new feelings and add them well,
Bake well with a load of loyalty,
Serve to a nation with a coat of care.

Nicola Mackintosh (11)
Abraham Moss High School

TWIN TOWERS

We all saw the disaster
That was made by the master
From the Twin Towers
Mothers were shattered
Buildings were battered
Children cried
Firemen tried
People prayed
Bodies were laid
Jobs were lost
Countries crossed
America nearly perished
Afghanistan has already finished
The war has started
Air space has been granted
World War III
We might just be free.

Diana Nkomo (11)
Abraham Moss High School

ONCE I WAS FREE

I am a bird,
High in the sky,
Soaring with the clouds,
Singing out loud.

My wings were spread out,
Strong and safe,
Beating a solid rhythm,
Like I was running a race.

Swooping and swaying
Without a care in the world
Narrowly missing a man
Who was greying.

The sky grew grey,
Black clouds appeared
The sound of bird cries
Filled my eyes.

I flew faster and faster
Anxious with fear
Danger was very near.
Bang! The cries grew louder.

Louder with fear
Bang! Pain ran through my body
To the tip of my tail.
My mind was full of fear
Fear of what was next.

I was once independent,
I was once me,
I once felt like I was free.

But now I was falling
Falling and crying
I fell to the ground
Everything went black.

Syrah Shah (13)
Abraham Moss High School

THE ROAR OF THE TIGER

In the depth of the jungle
Where the tiger lurks around.
Tigers, I heard you,
Roaring.

Your miserable gloomy faces
Looking up at us, pleading.
We would make you a victim.
Roaring to your family
Just amongst the hills.
Tigers, I heard you,
Crying.

Your puzzled-looking faces
Your scent upon our noses
Tigers, I heard you,
Moaning.

Instead of life we choose
Tiger fur for our warmth
Your meat to prevent our hunger.
No doubt we will soon hear the news,
That you don't exist any longer!

Janine Armstrong (13)
Abraham Moss High School

A Recipe For Friendship

Take two dear friends that have destroyed their friendship
And are now in a vulnerable and miserable state!
Crumble down the Dursleys' nastiness.
Mix in together some consideration and compromise,
Wish in honesty and happiness, extract out the miserable attitude,
Weigh up a ton of companionship.
Wash out thoroughly all the contempt and the hostility
Towards each other.
Sprinkle in a handful of patience and faith.
Mix with reliability and responsibility.
Spread a beautiful environment with a pinch of honesty.
Bake with modesty. Serve with elegance and tenderness,
Sincerity and hope.

Taweel Sohail (13)
Abraham Moss High School

A RECIPE FOR LOVE

Take a world that has been spoiled by hatred,
Crumble it in a bowl.
Add a large amount of love, whisk in joy and hope.
Take out all the hatred and greed.
Weigh up a thousand tons of happiness.
Wash down the sink all the anger.
Try to pick out all greed, anger and misery.
Separate nastiness from intolerance, stir well.
Put the mixture into a tin and bake in a moderate oven
                                        for a century.
Garnish with happiness, understanding and helpfulness.
Serve with trust and an open heart.

Alshafia Rahman (13)
Abraham Moss High School

RECIPE FOR PEACE

Take a part of the world which has cruelty and hate,
Pull them out, crumble it in a bowl.
Add a large jug of helpfulness, whisk in joy and love.
Shake out the terrorism and the bad things,
Weigh up a million tonnes of love and kindness,
Wash down the racism and sprinkle in a handful
                                of trust and friendship.
Take out all the weapons used in wars.
Add some tolerance,
A few ounces of humour would give a good flavour, stir well.
Put the mixture into a tin and bake in a moderate oven for a year.

Janey Shahid (12)
Abraham Moss High School

THE MOON

A sphere of white and silver sailing along the black shores,
Swiftly sailing, gradually gliding above our heads.
It's a light or diamond to sparkle in the night-time sky,
To light the way to sailors lost at sea.
The only face that has been there forever,
The stories it can tell.
It will unravel itself like a ball of wool,
To share its life with all who care.

Louise Gee (14)
Booth Hall Hospital School

MOON

The moon is resting above so high
Still in the night it stands,
Lighting up the clouds it commands,
Shining like a huge star it stands.
Moonlight beams peep through trees so dim.

Kieran Partington (15)
Booth Hall Hospital School

THE EYE OF THE DEVIL

The moon is like a ball of fire
Wildly moving like barbed wire
The edges are sharp like a machete blade
Will this devil moon ever fade?

Robert Harrison (15)
Booth Hall Hospital School

PIE

Andy Pyre loves to lie
He has never eaten a pie
His dad always wears a tie
His hairdresser's about to die
Andy's mate never cries
When fatty Fudge eats his pies.
Meat and potato, apple, cherry
Summer fruit that's a lot.
Meat, cheese and onion, beef
All the pies can't fit in a pot.
Andy's mate should have a lock
For his pies
A tin with room for his stock
Mrs Butler stares into space
Fatty Fudge is stuffing his face
He has a face so big it could be a base,
A pizza base that is.
Nick made a new pizza
It looked like his sister Lisa
Andy caught a virus
Its name was Tirus
The doctor said the only cure;
It's worth a try
He must eat of piece of pie!

Callum Palmer (12)
Booth Hall Hospital School

HAPPINESS

To be happy is a wondrous feeling,
the world becomes bright and your load light.

To be happy is a splendid feeling
you feel airy and light like a bird in flight.
Oh to be happy.

No one can make you happy as can no item,
your happiness is in you!
You are your happiness . . . to be happy.

To be happy, that is what I desire,
I would brave the deepest oceans and the highest fires . . .

Yet at the end of the day I sit and I think . . .
I'm lucky, because I'm me and you're lucky
because you're you,
help others and do your best,
live your life and be a success,
but at the end of it all you never find true happiness,
happiness is your Holy Grail, you can seek it forever
but it will never be found.

But at the end of the day, be happy you tried.

Kyle Robb (14)
Burnage High School For Boys

I'M LOOKING FOR A FRIEND

I'm looking for a best friend,
someone just like me,
someone good at football,
someone smart and free . . .
I'm looking for someone special
someone really clever,
someone rich and true . . .
Yes, I'm looking for a new friend
to do the things I like
that special kind of person
that person could be you.

Tariq Akram (12)
Burnage High School For Boys

WHY DOES NO ONE LOVE ME?

Why does no one love me?
Is it because I'm me?
Is it because I'm ugly?
Is it because I have ginger hair
Or is it because of my annoying stare?

Why does no one love me?
Is it because of the way I speak?
Is it because I'm very weak?
Is it because I'm easily taught
Or is it because I'm dead, dead short?

Why does no one love me?
Is it because I'm really bright?
Is it because I do not fight?
It is because I like school
Or is it simply I'm not cool?

So could someone please answer my question,
'Why does no one love me?'

Stephen Bryson-Taylor (14)
Burnage High School For Boys

IT'S ME, THE MOON

It's me,
The moon, I'm
all alone, unlike Mercury,
Who moans and moans. It's me
The moon, relaxed and calm, unlike
Mars who rages with alarm. It's me the
Moon, watch me smile, as the stars still
Glow, for miles and miles. It's me the
Moon, I watch at night, I sleep all
day, when it is light. It's me the
Moon, I'm fast asleep, I
Close my eyes and
Never peep.

Louise Elton (11)
Fairfield High School

SPRING

Spring arrives,
a flower is born,
it grows its petals
from dusk to dawn.

It blows in the wind,
the petals fall,
they float to the ground
like a feather off a wall.

Nathan Gilbert (12)
Newall Green High School

ROAD SAFETY

My mum bought me a bike
and said take a hike.
She bought me a helmet
some pads and a bell.
'Now go outside and ride like hell.'
She watched me ride so smooth and swell.

Daniel Williams (13)
Newall Green High School

HOMEWORK

Homework, homework there
We have no weekend
But the teachers don't care
English, science, I do them all
We do that much I miss football.

Kieran Raynes (12)
Newall Green High School

DEVON

The quiet countryside
at the end of the British Isles
which has its ups
and had its downs.
The foot and mouth
has ruined its reputation
but the locals know best
that the twists in the roads
aren't that bad,
that the clouds in the sky
aren't that low,
the tormented hills
which have been
ruffled and shuffled
from side to side
amaze me that they have been
there from season to season,
year to year.
When I leave one year
I wonder for the next year,
will the clouds in the sky
still be low.
Will the twists in the roads
still hurt your neck
going round the corners.
But all in all
I never worry for a minute!

Thomas Barclay (12)
Newall Green High School

DO YOU WANT TO BE A WITCH?

Do you want to be a witch
you'll need a pointed hat,
a long black cloak and
a little black cat.
You'll need a magic potion,
you'll need a wand too,
if you want to be a witch
there's lots you'll have to do.

Stephanie Green (12)
Newall Green High School

BATH TIME

Come 8 o'clock on Sunday night,
is a night, I love all right.
I soak in my bath for over an hour
and end up smelling like a flower.

I love to fill it with bubbles to the brim,
then I can't wait to jump right in.
To relax and soak all day,
I feel my troubles just float away.

When my mum comes to shout,
I really don't want to get out.
I am all ready, wrinkly like a prune,
But my bath time ends too soon.

Kelsey Latimer (12)
Newall Green High School

I Am Happy

Biting cold
With a fist in my face,
Warm at last
Blood trickling down my face,
My stomach empty as a haunted house,
Growling like a dying lion.

Warm again
She thumped the door into my face,
I am happy as a baby I have my own cupboard now,
The blood is starting to congeal
Finally I have got something to play with,
Finally my stomach is full
I have devoured the leftovers from the dog's dinner.

Hand hard as a stone
My right arm is no more,
I am happy she has lit the door,
Flames flickered,
I am happy,
I am with the angels now

Finally I am happy!

Nathan Robinson
Newall Green High School

THE TRAIN JOURNEY

I'm on the train, I have a seat,
When a man said to me, 'I have sore feet.'
I let him sit in my place,
So I had to move up another space.

The train goes fast, the train goes slow,
The train passes through sleet and snow.
Now through a tunnel as dark as night,
Now out of the tunnel in a flash of light.

Then comes a train with empty trucks,
That never go too fast,
Its driver man has always time
To wave and say goodbye.

Stephanie Matthews (11)
Newall Green High School

DREAMS

As I rub my tired eyes,
And force my heavy lids open.
I try to recall what I dreamed of,
Last night when the moon was high.

I dreamt of a place when the sun did shine,
And everyone was happy.
The world was such a perfect place
Last night when the moon was high.

Kerry Matthews (14)
Newall Green High School

ALONE

In the middle of a crowded room
There is a child in the gloom.
The music is deafening
She doesn't move.
People talk to her, she doesn't hear
Instead she stares at them with a blank expression
Not knowing this girl is in a deep depression.
She never seems to smile for long
People think she's just a moody so and so
But if they knew the hurt she feels
They too would know the way her longing heart reels.

Samantha Deveney (15)
Newall Green High School

LOVE

There is a boy in the year above
Who is my one and only true love
He is good-looking and cool
And, oh boy he rules!
He is smart and funny
Oh why can't I be his honey.
I wish he would feel the same way as me
But this obviously means it shouldn't be!

Louise Moss (15)
Newall Green High School

MY NAN

My nan comes to see me every week,
But really I don't know how she's got the cheek!
She walks in, sits down and gives me the most painful-looking frown
With her awful voice yelling, 'Make me a brew!'
Quickly I think of an excuse, 'Orr Nan, I can't, I've got the flu!'
As she stands up with her immense glasses,
Oh my God my water passes, she grabs my ear,
'For God's sake, Nan I can't hear.'
'Don't be cruel,' she whispers, 'to your old loving nan,
Make me a brew and a fry-up in the pan!'

Laura Wallace (14)
Newall Green High School

BOB

I looked at my watch, three days, seven hours, twenty-four minutes,
forty-nine seconds. I cheated on him, well that's what he reckons.

I looked at my watch, three days, seven hours, twenty-four minutes,
fifty-four seconds. With his best mate, well that's what he reckons.

It was Friday night, when he walked in, he sure got a fright.
When he turned on the light. I cheated on him, well he was right!

It was his best mate Bob, he saw us together and started to sob.
So the mobile phone that he did lob, that was the end of his
best mate Bob.

Leanne Baker (14)
Newall Green High School

GHYLL HEAD

At Ghyll Head, there's plenty to see,
It's especially good with Jacqui Lee.
There's only one games room, which is OK
When you play pool, you don't have to pay.
At the night, you will have a ball,
Then watch Curtis kick through a wall.
At half seven Sir wakes you up,
So we went downstairs and put tea in a cup.
After breakfast, we went mountaineering,
Sounds of the wind, it's what we were hearing.
Then we went back, time for tea,
I sat next to Rob and a boy called Lee.
The tea looked like sick, we just sat on our seats
Then we ran upstairs and ate Lee's sweets.
The night was near and we played manhunt
Rob went after Caroline, I wouldn't.
In the lounge, Rob was staring at Caroline,
So they both went out for some wine
Debbie looked at me, I gave her a glance
She came over to me and asked me to dance,
On the minibus, I sat near Jacqui Lee,
Oh lucky, lucky, lucky me.

Christopher O'Keefe (14)
Newall Green High School

OUTSIDE

The sky is blue
The birds are singing
It's a wonderful day
Outside walking around.
The grass is green
The sun is shining
Outside walking around.
The clouds are coming
But nothing stops me smiling
Outside walking around.
Oh no, it's raining
But I keep on smiling
While I am outside walking around.

Michelle Bradburn (14)
Newall Green High School

LISA

My name is Lisa,
I am fourteen years old,
I love the sunshine,
I hate the cold.

My best friend is called Sam,
She is really great,
There is nothing about her
That I hate.

I hate politics,
I hate war,
Why can't we live happy,
This life's a bore.

I love my father,
I love my mother,
I am not so fond of my brother.

Sam thinks she's a fish,
I think chicken
Is the world's best dish.

My grandad died when I was five,
Oh how I wish he was still alive,
There is no one like him on this Earth,
More than my life alone he is worth.

Lisa Mealing (14)
Newall Green High School

PEOPLE

People are really strange things,
I wonder where they all come from,
Not many people know,
Some think it was a massive explosion
Like a great big bomb.

People are all so different,
Short, tall, fat or thin,
To start to describe all these people,
You wouldn't know where to begin.

All these different people,
Reproduced on the world today,
Thousands of millions all over the place,
All going their own different way.

Thousands of people all walking around,
In their own ways and paces
Why are there so many people
All different sizes and races.

Lots of people moaning and groaning
Sometimes playing their little games
But when you really think of it
We're not different, we're all really the same.

Jade-Fay Rowland (14)
Newall Green High School

MY SPECIAL PLACE

If I had a special place;
I know just where it'd be,
Me and the sunshine,
No us, just me,
It'd be so peaceful,
To be up above,
To swim with the stars,
That twinkle with love,
I'd sit on the stars,
I'd cry on the moon,
I'd sleep on the sun,
And it would be so much fun,
I would be free,
Just like a bird,
And there'd be
A sea of warm sunshine
All for me
How nice this would be
To sunbathe under stars
To linger in the sky
I would tell you my special place
But I can't, it's mine.

Jayde Maguire (14)
Newall Green High School

LITTLE FIGHTERS

Arrows fly across this place
Guns and grenades lay it to waste
Aliens visit from far-off places
There are monsters from a hundred races
Through this place soldiers scatter
Scary things with teeth that chatter
But if you look closely and quietly creep
You can find mighty heroes fast asleep
They control all the mayhem in this place
But for now they sleep soundly with an innocent face
With courage they have faced all kinds of dire foes
And laid them under with knives, guns and bows
Just now they're tired, so in twilight's gloom
We just close the door on our little ones' room
Let them sleep soundly till morning's new light
Brings them more battles and monsters to fight.

Sarah Shelmerdine (14)
Newall Green High School

SNOOKER DAY

The cue strikes the ball,
       there's silence in the hall.
The reds are down the pocket,
       as fast as a rocket.
Then goes the yellow,
       there's a really loud bellow.
Then the green goes down,
       following that is the brown.
With a hit of the cue,
       down goes the blue.
What about the pink,
       that's next in the link.
Follows that is the black,
       and then comes . . .
Clap, clap, clap.

Dean Gowrie (15)
Newall Green High School

IF I WON THE LOTTERY

If I won the lottery
What would I do?
I'd buy a red Ferrari
Maybe even two.

I'd buy a huge mansion
And invite all my friends,
We'd have a big pool party,
That never ever ends!

Perhaps go to America
And visit Disneyland,
Then off to Hawaii
To lie on the golden sand.

Searching through designer shops
To buy all I can see,
I know I've bought enough
But no one can stop me.

I'd have my own theme park
With lots of thrilling rides,
I'd also have a swimming pool
With big swirly slides.

If I won the lottery . . .
Huh!
I can always dream!

Samantha Burns (12)
Newall Green High School

HALLOWE'EN

Ten minutes past the midnight hour
The midnight's moon turns green and sour.
Three witches come out to play
And the ghoulies are here to stay.
Darkness surrounds all the graveyard
To not be afraid you'll be so hard.
The witches cast an evil spell
So everyone there would smell like hell.
The Hallowe'en hours are nearly over
The witches ride off into the night.
The ghoulies start to fade from sight.
Hallowe'en is going away
Daylight is now here to stay.

Paul Meehan (12)
Newall Green High School

E-MAIL ME JOE!

I type in my letter, then click 'send',
I've sent it to Joe, my e-mail friend.
I quietly sit and wait for a reply,
It's not come yet, I wonder why.
It's been five minutes and still nothing yet,
Do you suppose he might forget?
Of course not, it couldn't be,
Or maybe he's found someone better than me.
He e-mails me everyday,
In his own unique, special way.
I guess it's now time to face,
There's no one else to take his place.
Just before I say goodnight,
The name Joe caught my sight.
Finally my e-mail came,
'Sorry, it's late, I was watching the game.'
Typical excuse for a boy,
I must admit I was filled with joy.
I guess this must be the end,
But I've got Joe, my e-mail friend.

Hannah Cummings (12)
Newall Green High School

THE BLUSHING FACE

Who is God?
My father of all time.
What is the sun?
My rage and anger.
Where is Heaven?
The place above my head.
What is romance?
Romeo and Juliet.
How is life on the Milky Way?
A chocolate bar for me everyday.
What is the ring on Saturn?
Cold, frozen ice.
What is anger?
A fire inside of you.
Is life a dream?
Mine is.

Aaron Fairhurst (12)
Newall Green High School

FOOTY

Footy's good,
Footy's fine,
Lots of mud,
That ball's mine,
Shout for it,
Get a kick,
Oops-a-daisy, what a trip,
Spot kick,
Score a goal,
Andy Cole,
What a goal!

Ben Carroll (13)
Newall Green High School

SUMMER

Summer is coming
Spring has gone,
The bluebirds are humming
It's time for fun.

The sun is shining
The sky is blue,
The wind is whining
The cows go moo.

I'm lying on grass,
It's great to be warm,
On my doggy dog Lass
The flees form.
I'm dark and tan
Not white anymore.

The red sunburn
Is getting sore.
The sun is setting, it's time to go
I'm in bed now, alone and low.

Ruth Egbe (12)
Newall Green High School

WHEN YOU LOSE A FRIEND

When you lose a friend,
The loss is hard to bear.
A friend who's always been there,
You're both as stubborn as each other,
None of you want to apologise first,
Instead you leak out your heart to your mother.
But if you carry on you'll lose her forever.
You jump suddenly off your seat,
You grab the phone,
And at the same time, blurt out . . .
'I'm sorry!'

Tegan Walker (13)
Newall Green High School

My Pen Pal Romance

My love is charming also sweet,
But yet we still have to meet.
My heart is pounding and even more
When your letter comes through the door.
I know what you look like but not for sure
Could there be less or even more?

I'm guessing you're thinking nearly the same,
Or are you hanging your head in shame.
I hope you haven't lied my dear
Or I'll have to shed a tear.

When will we meet? Oh make it soon,
I wrote and asked you, you said, 'Around noon.'
I waited at the station and an hour passed,
I've seen you arriving at long last.
We seemed to talk for ever and ever
I said, I wanted you to stay forever,
Then he said, 'You're no longer my pen pal friend,
But my soulmate until the end.'

Megan Miller (12)
Newall Green High School

SEASONS

Winter is a time when wasps whoosh away,
Trees stand naked, laden with silver frost,
People dash around with stone-cold faces,
Spring banishes the bleakness of winter,
The garden awakes with the warming sun,
The aura of spring brings meadows to life,
Summer arrives with strawberries and cream,
Children licking lollies by the seaside,
Autumn rushes in with golden brown leaves,
Geese fly south with the memory of summer.

Alexander Holleran (12)
Newall Green High School

LONG LIVE AMERICA

There was a devastating tragedy a couple of weeks ago,
Were they friend or foe?
The great planes of America were taken down with their pride,
People were horrified,
Even sick,
So what made them tick?
Bush's brain is ticking,
We will be shifting them off the planet if we find out who,
And he doesn't care what they do.
Britain has helped by giving need
To the people that don't do greed.
The terrorists have won the battle but not the war,
Long live America,
I hope you win in your time of need!

James Darbyshire (12)
Newall Green High School

PRISONER

I am a prisoner locked in here,
I am a prisoner full of fear,
I stay in my cell
For most of the night
Pray to God to
Help me fight.
I tried to slit my wrists
One night
But my cellmate came in
And saved my life.

I'm counting the days,
I'm counting the weeks,
It feels like I've got ten years
But I've only got twenty-one weeks.

I am a prisoner locked in here
Will somebody please take away
My fear.

Lisa Manso (13)
Newall Green High School

OCEAN

Blue is the colour of the ocean
Filled with life and always in motion
It's long, it's deep, it's tantalisingly sleek
From fish to whales and even board sails.
She's wet, she's cold, she's very, very old,
Blue is the colour of the ocean.

Damien Burrows (14)
Newall Green High School

WINNIE THE POOH

Winnie the Pooh and Tigger too,
Rabbit, Piglet, Kanga and Roo.

Honey and trees, covered in bees,
everyone is saying 'Honey please!'

When Winnie is on his thinking spot
he likes to eat out of his hunny pot.

When we say bye to Christopher Robin,
Winnie the Pooh is always sobbing.

Heather O'Connor (13)
Newall Green High School

AUTUMN

The autumn leaves drift past my window
The autumn leaves of red and gold
Children on their way to school
Scrape their feet along the kerb
Collecting them as they go.

Ker-plunk is the sound of the conkers,
As they fall from the tree to the earth,
Entombed in their green prickly shell,
Or opened to expose their reddy-brown nut.

As the days get shorter
The dark nights come upon us but get longer,
And the rain pours down
And the wind howls like a wolf at a full moon.

'Trick or treat? yell the children,
As they knock on the doors of their neighbours
Faces painted as terrifying demons and ghosts
Costumes of witches on their brooms
Little innocent faces peering out asking for sweets.

Whoosh! It's Bonfire Night, rockets dart across the sky,
Like a shooting star in the dark night,
Gatherings of people surrounding the bonfire,
Children with their hats, scarves and gloves protecting themselves,
They write their names with sparklers
And when they're gone plunge them into icy water.

And then one day as the city awakes, ice on the windows
And smoke coming out of mouths when breathing,
Frost glistening on the grass and suddenly it's winter!

Andrew Fisher (13)
Newall Green High School

BOYS

Boys are really noisy
Driving their cars
Eating and drinking
Smoking a cigar

They go to the pub
To watch their favourite sport
Screaming and shouting
Football galore.

Hayley Barker (13)
Newall Green High School

INFORMATION TECHNOLOGY VERSUS MISS WILSON

If I ripped off an unknown poet
Would Miss Wilson ever know it?
There must be millions of poems on the Internet
So ripping one off is a pretty safe bet.
And Miss Wilson wouldn't discover me
She's got more chance of winning the lottery
And I'll get a good grade for my poetry
Even though it wasn't written by me.

But hold on a minute, say I'm discovered,
Say one of my friends blows my cover
Tells Miss Wilson 'Boyley's a pleb
He stole his poem off the World Wide Web.'
I doubt if I'd be teacher's pet,
In fact Miss Wilson might get upset,
Because I was too lazy to write a poem myself
And had to pinch one off someone else.

So I put pen to paper, not finger to key
And my English teacher gets an original from me.
It might not be Shakespeare or Rudyard Kipling
But I had a lot of fun composing this thing.
This poetry writing; it isn't half bad
And I discovered a talent I didn't know I had.
I like making up rhymes and making them scan
From now on I'm John Boyle the poetry man.

John Boyle (13)
Newall Green High School

A Watery Night's Tale

Swish, sway,
The water was coming,
Swimming around,
Curving the ground,
Meandering around corners,
Faster and faster,
The water rose,
But not making a sound,
No, it's too clever for that,
The sly water,
Slowly rising and rising,
Growing and growing,
Higher and higher,
Then, in a sudden swish . . .
It was all over,
And then . . .
Not a sound,
The water was swimming around,
Not a care in the world,
Waiting,
Waiting for its next victim.

Jenny Fisher (13)
Newall Green High School

MAN U ARE THE BEST!

I got off the bus, had finally arrived.
I took a quick glare then stepped inside.
The stadium was colossal and stood way up high,
and the top of it merged into the cerulean sky.
All the fans walked and went to their chairs
but soon would stand like really cold hairs.
The smell of pies twisted across the air,
but the match would soon start, so I didn't care.
The fans all shouted and their shirts were immense,
my fists became tight and I became very tense.
The players walked out like brave men to war,
and all the United fans began to scream and roar.

'Man U! Man U!' Best team in the world
but when I heard 'City!' My toes went and curled.
The match kicked off and we were 3-1 up!
But I sat back down and drank from my cup.
The final whistle went and I looked up,
8-3! 8-3! - We weren't in the muck.
My eyes glistened, I was so proud.
And I showed my love by screaming out loud.
But now I had to leave but I was so glad.
I bet that result made City mad!

Robert Schofield (14)
Newall Green High School

POEM

United win The Premiership every year
The crowd go demented with joy.
All the players are on the pitch
Celebrating with delight.
They're always in the spotlight
There are always plenty of goals
Always never concede
They're in Europe next year
They've won The Premiership
That is the reason.
They will win Europe next season.

Richard Caine (13)
Newall Green High School

PERFUME OF DEATH

Come, take a whiff or a slight sniff
For I am the perfume of deception
I will capture your body, capture your mind
And invade your emotions until they are blind

I will capture your brain and drive you insane
You will become an insignificant slave
If you are brave I'll put you in your grave
Sooner than you know

I'll form a hand large and grand
And throttle your last breath of existence
I'm a strong-smelling aroma, try to resist me
For I am the perfume of death.

Paul Daly (14)
Newall Green High School

ONE BIG APPLE CRUMBLE

Everything's rubble
Everything's trash
Looking for bodies is always bad
We watch them fight
Each day and night
And we are wishing
They will be alright.

Searching the rubble
Searching the bricks
It looks like they need
A box of tricks
They're getting nowhere
They never do
Because they are the victims
And we are not.

Those terrible men
That caused all this
Are drinking champagne
And think suffering is bliss.

Michael McCaffery (13)
Newall Green High School

AUTUMN LEAVES

The last leaf on the tree takes its fall,
The trees are naked but still stand tall.
Jack Frost comes out for his morning walk,
Curling his icy fingers around the flower's stalk.
Children walk through golden leaves,
Wrapped up warm against the autumn breeze.
The flowers have packed up, they've gone away,
To rise again on a summer's day.
Morning brings a fine, misty rain,
Oh no! It's drizzling again.
The birds are ready, ready to fly,
To leave behind the dreary, grey sky.

Melissa Tennant (14)
Newall Green High School

SPOOKY RAP

When I woke up in the night
and I got a little fright
Oh yeah!

I saw a shadow on the wall
I hadn't seen it all before
Oh yeah!

I heard a knock on my door
I heard a creak on the floor
Oh yeah!

Is there someone under my bed
'cause I know I'm . . .
Dead!

Leanne Berry (12)
Newall Green High School

POP

Pop in
Pop out
Pop over the road
Pop out for a walk
Pop in for a talk
Pop down to the shop
Can't stop,
Got to pop.

Zoe McCarthy (12)
Newall Green High School

MY SISTER ABBIE

I've got a sister, her name is Abbie
She gets in a mess and sometimes looks shabby.
She screams and she cries, she never keeps still.
Her nappy is runny, whenever she's ill.
Her hair is blonde, her eyes are blue.
She can say lots of words like 'Mummy' and 'shoe'.
She is often a terror and has tantrums and fits.
I think that she drives my mum out of her wits.
She is almost two years old and looks like her dad.
My other sister Jess, makes her get mad.
They squabble and argue, they fuss, they fight.
She punches, she scratches, she headbutts and bites.
I ignore all the crying and stamping of feet
Because my sister Abbie is gorgeous and sweet.

Faye Leaver (13)
Newall Green High School

IN THE PUB

I went in a pub,
had a laugh and a joke,
had a look around and saw some weird bloke.

He was smoking a cig,
and looked at me weird,
I didn't like him,
or his long beard.

I told my friend,
She said, 'Ignore him.
He's a scruff and lives in a bin.'
I turned to look at him,
I said, 'Oh no, where did he go?'
All my friend said was 'I don't know.'

Sarah Davies (12)
Newall Green High School

MY FRIGHT IN THE NIGHT

I woke up in the night
and I got a little fright.

I saw a shadow on my wall
I thought it was my brother Paul.

Can you see the rope around your neck?
You look a total wreck.

Now you're hanging from the ceiling
you should know the feeling.

Laura Marino (12)
Newall Green High School

ROSE

There was a young girl named Rose,
Who had a large wart on her nose.
When she had it removed,
Her nose was improved
But her glasses slipped down to her toes.

Laura Hampson (12)
Newall Green High School

SILENCE
*(Dedicated to all those people who lost
their lives on the 11th September 2001
in New York and Washington)*

The wind ain't howling
The birds don't sing
The dogs aren't growling
The bells don't ring

The owls aren't hooting
The clocks don't chime
The guns aren't shooting
The poets don't rhyme

The cars aren't beebing
The snakes don't hiss
The frogs aren't leaping
The couples don't kiss

The radio isn't booming
The telly's not loud
There is no shouting from a crowd

There is no alcohol

There is no violence

The whole world is
                    in complete
                              silence.

Emma Jayne Scott (11)
Newall Green High School

MY BROTHER IS A TEENAGER

My brother is a teenager,
he thinks he's so cool.
He has to be perfect every day for school.
If there's one spot dangling from his face
he will go blood-red and jump up into space.
He will walk around the house in vain,
and I'll mumble, 'What a pain!'
He takes a year getting dressed
making sure he looks his best.

Shadelle Logan (12)
Newall Green High School

BULLY

They do it all the time
they're never out of trouble.
They always commit a crime
their mates call 'em double trouble.
It's not paradise 'cause it is hell.
Do the names Mike and Ryan ring a bell?
This is a rhyme that they sing
'Bullies, bullies, what do we do?
Bullies, bullies, we hit, pick and bully you.'

Charlotte Hoarey (11)
Newall Green High School

THE BEST TEAM IN THE WORLD

We're always in the Premiership.
We will never go down.
We are the best team in Europe.
We can beat any team in any town.
We can win any cup.
We can kick the ball, then score.
We can beat any opponent.
We have got a lot of skill.
We have the best goalie.
We have the best team.
    Who are we?

Manchester United!

Marcus Ely (12)
Newall Green High School

THE COLD NIGHT

It is winter without snow, but very cold indeed
with Father Christmas coming the next day.
Wind howling very fast against the houses.

Then Santa comes and it starts snowing
whilst the wind is blowing
and Santa comes down the chimney very fast
as fast as lightning on the cold winter's night.

And next time Christmas comes, watch out
for Santa and say hello from me.

Bradley Thomas (11)
Newall Green High School

LOVE SCHOOL

There was a school in Devon,
Which was pretty much like Heaven,
There was a rule,
That you must always be cool,
Which was made up by Miss McDemeven.

Another one was in France,
Where you could sing, play and dance,
There was no lesson,
There was no depression,
The school was owned by Miss Lance.

But the favourite was in the middle of Spain,
Where the inside of the school could rain;
You could drench all the teachers,
Especially Miss Features
And knock down the school with a crane.

Jayne Cookson (12)
Newall Green High School

BOYFRIENDS

Boyfriends are always up to no good.
All they think about are guts and blood,
They are always hanging about with the boys,
Or playing with other big boys' toys,
They are always trying to make an impression,
Thinking they are cool by missing a lesson.

Then finally at the end of the day,
You long to hear 'I love you,'
But no, they say:

'You're finished!'

'You're finished,'
Well I guess it ends,
Well I guess that's the look you get
    with
                    Boyfriends!

Elizabeth Baker (11)
Newall Green High School

THE BUG

One day I felt sick
My mum thought I thought she was thick
I said 'No school.'
My mum said 'You're a fool.'
She thought I was lying
Although I was dying.
She made me go to school
How very cruel!
I couldn't eat my dinner
In the race I wasn't a winner.
I got a lot of detention
For not paying attention.
In the baths I nearly drowned
All the teachers frowned.
Eventually I went home
It was like entering a pleasure dome.
I could finally go to bed
Oh my aching head!

Daniel Boyle (11)
Newall Green High School

WHO?

He's big, fat, round and yellow
he has a red top and eats honey?

It's Winnie the Pooh!

He's small, pink and has big pink
ears, but is scared of the dark?

It's Piglet!

He's big and purple and always
loses his tail?

It's Eeyore!

He's big and orange and also has black stripes
and he likes to bounce on his tail?

It's Tigger!

Holly Dowd (11) & Stephanie Mellor (12)
Newall Green High School

COMETS

I saw a comet
late last night.
It hit me in the face
and gave me a fright.

Comets come big
Comets come small
Comets kill all.

I woke up last night
and saw a comet on the floor
it had knocked me
through the door.

Nicholas Dowd (11)
Newall Green High School

THE RAINY DAY

I woke up in the morning
And heard the falling rain.
Oh no, I thought to myself
I'm stuck in the house again.

I watched out of the window
And saw puddles on the ground.
The pitter-patter on the windowpane,
Such a miserable sound.

I wish the rain would go away
And the sun would shine once more,
But looking at those big, black clouds,
I'm stuck inside for sure.

Matthew Campbell (11)
Newall Green High School

THE WIND

The wind likes to blow,
Like a raging bulldog,
It likes to run and go,
In the winter's cold fog.

The wind likes to hover,
Like the clouds in the sky,
I don't know why it bothers,
I don't know why.

The wind likes to fly,
Like the heavens above,
To meet his girlfriend Tie,
To make true love.

The pair of the winds,
Live happily together
And have loads of kids,
Forever and ever.

They call one Shower,
One Droplet, one Breeze
They all live together,
All together in threes.

Kelly Sherratt (11)
Newall Green High School

FOOTBALL MAD!

I love football, I watch it all the time,
Never a match missed, all I do is stare.
Man United, Liverpool and all the other teams,
Play against each other trying to win their dreams.

The European Cup, World Cup and all the others,
Teams working as hard as they can trying to win
the trophies.
Football! Football! Football again!
That's all I watch, it will always be the same!

Daniel Vickers (11)
Newall Green High School

WITCHES

Flying broomsticks in the sky,
Wicked potions of dead frog's eye.
Spells aplenty, curses too
All contained in the witches' brew.

Secluded cottages, pointed hats
Wizened smiles, jet-black cats
Cackles, shackles, screeches, yells,
The witches wake at midnight's bells.

The clock has struck 12 and the witches are up high,
Camouflaged well in the deep, dark sky,
Be careful, watch out when the witches are out,
For they can smell you with their rather large snout.

Melany Haslam (12)
St Monica's RC High School

ANIMALS

As my mum grows old,
So does the sun
The tigers get weaker
And the monkeys can't run.

But the sun still sets
As the tigers fall out
The monkeys climb trees
And my mum's still about.

But what the sun calls day
And the tigers call strong
The monkeys I hope, you live long.

Samantha Haslam (15)
St Monica's RC High School

ANIMALS

Animals' actions are meant to be funny
Like how some hop, for example, a bunny
And how the bees make their sweet honey
And how they play when it is sunny.

The bird (my favourite) soars up on high
Higher and higher and higher he'll fly
The baby birds, harder and harder they try
To glide like their parents, way up in the sky.

Where they live really puzzles me
Like dolphins that swim way down in the sea
And when the monkey swings through his tree
But it's nature's way, so let them be!

Corrinne Wilkinson (11)
St Monica's RC High School

THE GREAT WAR

The sky above the scar in the land,
Was black as the minds below.
No thought of any mercy,
Only a tension for the go.

The taste of fear was in the air,
The wire, dull and red
From early fools that followed the path
That he would surely tread.

The sign came as the whistle blew,
They charged to meet the foe.
The blood of him and his comrades
Began to stain the snow.

John Purdue (13)
St Monica's RC High School

MY MUM AND GODMOTHER: SUN

It had been the first time she'd
seen me since I was a baby.
She walked through the door and the
room filled with rays.
Her voice was warm, tender and loving.

Her arms curved around me like the
sun's light curves the Earth.
She spoke in a warm Irish accent, 'Hello Catherine.'
I replied just in the warm loving voice as she did.

The next hour or so passed quickly, like all the
planets revolving around the sun.
At every opportunity she could she stopped and
her arms curved around me again.
I don't remember her when I was younger, my godmother
that is, but it's as if I've known her all my life.

Day in, day out, everyone worships the sun.
How warm it is, how summery.
How bright and cheery.
My godmother and my mum always live for the moment.
At some stage in our lives we find someone we can
relate to. I'm lucky I have two, my mum and my godmother.

They share all of these statements.
I idolise them both.

Catherine Carrig (13)
St Monica's RC High School

UNISON IN WAR

I looked out at the starry night and saw the peaceful moon,
I saw the loving stars and knew it'd be over soon
Everyone waited, prayed and wished for an end,
But the wounds the war made would be difficult to mend
The war made a gash that was crooked and smeared
From the strongest to the weakest everyone feared
Even the bramble picker and the strawberry seeder
Even the little baby and his social service feeder
Even the smiling nun and baker
Even the priest and the candlestick maker
Even Sam and his work force of five
Even Jim, Ricky and the new boy Clive
Even the dumb, the blind and the deaf
Even Uncle Jimmy and Aunty Beth
Even the jailbreakers and the old bill
Even the carpenters and the man in the mill
Even the bad boy put in torture for us to see
Even the boy on the corner and lonely, sad little me
After the war the hurt and the fighting
People don't care much about thunder and lightning
And before the rain clears and the sun comes back
People go inside and just grab their mac
The rain is everywhere from Glasgow to Dover,
But it doesn't matter now the war is over.

Joel Moseley (14)
St Monica's RC High School

NATURE IN SEASONS

Nature is a way of life
Each and every day,
So when the seasons come along
Everyone is gay.

Autumn's when the leaves change colour
To orange, red and brown,
So all the crunching on the floor
Makes a very noisy sound.

Winter is a time of storms
And very icy nights,
But there is always Christmas time
And lots of snowball fights.

The first flowers of the year
Bloom as warmth returns,
Spring is heralded by swarming birds
And newly-budded ferns.

Summer brings the sun and rain
That sweep across the land,
It brightens up all creation
So let's give God a hand. *(clap, clap).*

Danielle Noone (13)
St Monica's RC High School

SPRING

A cold early morning in spring after a long
Night of rain,
And the early blossomed daffodils guard the
Long blades of fresh, green grass,
The cool morning breeze,
Dances elegantly through the trees,
And the large magpies pass.

When the sunset arrives in the pastel sky,
And the warm glistening sun slowly sleeps
In the tall, shadowy hills and rests until
The morning comes,
The evening birds twitter quietly to themselves,
And then return to their families,
In their homes.

Stephanie Porter (14)
St Monica's RC High School

ANIMALS

The eagle flew high in the air,
Soaring high without a care.
The eagle flew towards the sea,
Flying past, right over me.

The shark swam down very deep,
All the way down to 5,000 feet.
The creature sped up and chased its prey,
All the way down the deep, dark and grey.

The snake slithered across the sand.
Right across the sun-soaked land.
The snake rested under a stone,
And then went past some animal bones.

Richard Styles (13)
St Monica's RC High School

PEACE

Peace. Where did it go?
Love, they cried, friendship, let happiness fill the air,
There are people out there that really do care.
A symbol in our minds, it's more than that.
Fairies, flowers and forests full of magic.
This image we destroyed is ruined, oh so tragic!
What about the caring, sharing and helping others too,
The harmony, tranquillity, loving me, loving you!
Some people carry all of this, but some just ignore
The things that make the world a better place.
We're trapped inside a cage of war,
Oh, is there nothing we can do?

Sinead Fynes-Black (12)
St Monica's RC High School

PERSON IN THE MIRROR

I look at myself in the mirror,
But is it really me?
Is that what everyone else can see?

I look at myself in the mirror,
Who's this looking back at me?
Who is it inside?

I look at myself in the mirror,
And someone is looking back.
Are they trying to tell me something?
Maybe it's really me!

Shevonne Barstow (14)
St Monica's RC High School

THE WALL

One billion bricks high, one billion bricks wide,
I wonder what could be on the other side?
Maybe two pirate ships having a battle,
Or maybe a farmer feeding his cattle,
Maybe if you stepped over, you would get lost in time,
Or maybe it could be a poet writing a rhyme
Maybe some rabbits hopping in a field,
Or maybe a knight with a sword and a shield,
Maybe some apes swinging in the trees,
Or maybe a hive buzzing with bees,
Maybe a cavewoman feeding her child,
Or maybe it could just be my imagination
                             going wild . . .?

Emily Jackson (13)
St Monica's RC High School

WINTER

As nights grow longer
The winds go stronger
The days get short
What an awful thought!

The weather gets colder
As the trees look older
The snow comes down as flakes
It lies there 'til dawn breaks

People wrapped up nice and warm
As they remember when Christ was born
Children can't wait for their presents
As angels sing in the heavens.

Charlotte Spencer (13)
St Monica's RC High School

School

There are many types of people at school,
Some are geeks some are cool.
It all depends on who you know,
What you do and where you go.

When you go to school you get a name,
No one is normal, no one's the same.
School is just a popularity contest,
No one is level, someone has to be best.

Because of this people become neglected,
Always last to be chosen, never elected.
In this way school will never change,
Someone will always have the name Strange.

Niamh McKinstry (15)
St Monica's RC High School

MR BILL

A man of many moods, that's my friend Bill Tasker.
One day quite happy, the next, very sad.
His life is controlled by the amount of pain from his worn out hips.
He reminds me very much of a walrus with its shape and size,
With his busy moustache bristling as he sleeps in his chair.

When I look at him now it is hard to think of him as a young man,
He was a dancer of excellent quality, and could outshine
All others in the world of ballroom dancing.
Gaily skipping and dancing like a gazelle on the plains of Africa.

But due to the ravages of time and illness,
He has been reduced to being like a slow tortoise
Shuffling along with his two sticks.
But when we talk and joke together it's like
We are the same age and have the same sense of humour.
That's my friend, Mr Bill.

Jonathan Berry (13)
St Monica's RC High School

WINTER

In the winter when the snow falls
The children go out and play
They sledge and build snowmen with their friends
While the animals are tucked away.

Deep in their burrows the rabbits sleep on
Unaware of the fun on the hill.
The squeals and the shouts from the children above
Ring out despite the chill.

Rosina Fiorentini (15)
St Monica's RC High School

THE SPIDER'S WEB

Softly, silently, like a thief,
A phantom in the night.
Sits the spider dark and deadly
Spinning his web of shimmering light.
Backwards, forwards, up and down
He spins and weaves his silken crown.
Then, sits the spider, watching, waiting,
Swift to seize, to sting, to kill.

David Kendall (12)
St Monica's RC High School

THE WORLD I DREAMT OF

The world I dreamt of was full of joy,
Blessed with happiness and laughter,
But now I see there's no chance of that,
As the world is filled with anger.

The world I dreamt of was just like above,
It was tranquil, peaceful and good,
But now I know the real world,
Isn't full of love.

The world I dreamt of was understanding,
Beautiful and nice,
But now because of evil men,
Innocent children have paid the price.

Oh how I wished the world we lived in
Was harmonious and full of glee,
But I can only dream of this,
As it shall never be.

Andrew Sutton (13)
St Monica's RC High School

MY DOG SNOWY

My dog is called Snowy
He plays with a dog called Glowey
They hate the park,
They hate it because the other dogs bark,
Snowy and Glowey never fight,
Because they are bright.

Snowy has big feet,
He has these because he plays on the street.
He has a big tongue,
This is because he dreams of ping-pong,
He has a very big tail,
He always sweeps the snails and leaves
                        a very big trail.

Sean Cusack (12)
St Monica's RC High School

WEATHER

The elements show no mercy.
The wind numbs the snow and frost freezes,
the rain drowns and the sun scorches.
The elements show no mercy.
Silent is the sun-licking skin, red in a cool breeze.
Unnoticed.
Blind to the wind yet we hear and see her work.
Powerful is she.
Sheets of sprinkled silver is the breath of the Snow Queen.
Cruel, deadly and silent.
We see, hear and witness the rain as she weeps tears
of sorrow for mankind.
Floods are her punishment.
The elements show no mercy.

Fiona Coleman (14)
St Monica's RC High School

A FLAME

A flame is born with the strike of a match,
Just like a baby chick being hatched,
It seems to have an everlasting bright light,
Brightening up the darkest night,
It seems the flame will last forever,
Glowing through the dullest weather,
A young child's eyes watch surprised,
Wondering why the flame never dies,
The light's still shining all around,
The flame will never make a sound,
With one small blow the room is blackened,
While a teary-eyed child wonders what has happened.

Tabitha Wardle (16)
St Monica's RC High School

PEACE

Where is the peace?
Throughout love and hate
Coincidence and fate
Throughout rich and poor
Peacetime and war
Throughout prayer and anger
On the aeroplane hangar
The goods they carry matter
The soldiers' feet as they patter
No one knows the truth
As no one shows the proof
Where is the peace?

Where is the trust?
Does anyone know?
Can anyone show
Who is to blame
For the misunderstood game?
Is peace at hand?
As people demand
For love on this Earth
What is it worth?
Hearts are broken
Heartless words are spoken
Where is the trust?

Charlene Halstead (15)
St Monica's RC High School

IF ONLY . . .

Everywhere around us there could be
A world of love, peace and harmony.
A place where people get on with each other,
And treat each person like a sister or brother.

Instead every day around us we witness
A world full of hate and unhappiness.
A place where people struggle to stay alive,
And each new day is a fight to survive.

Our world shouldn't have to go on like this
This place should be a world of bliss.
For no good can come out of all this war
So what is all the fighting for?

Everywhere around us there could be
A world of love, peace and harmony.
We just have to try and find
A place in our hearts to be peaceful and kind.

Ashlie Goldman (14)
St Monica's RC High School

FLIGHT OF A DOVE

The white dove flew
through the deep blue sky,
over a calm sea,
as it reached an oasis.

The white dove flew
through the thunderstorm,
over a rough sea,
as it reached Ireland.

The white dove flew
through the colourful rainbow,
as it joined the two countries together.
A symbol of peace, a gift from God.

Natalie Hinett (15)
St Monica's RC High School

WAITING FOR YOU!

I'm waiting, hoping you still want me,
I'm waiting, hoping you still care.
I'm waiting, hoping you'll ask me.
I'm waiting, hoping you thought the first
kiss meant everything.
Did it? Well, it did for me.
I'm waiting, hoping that when you
told me you loved me, you meant it.
I'm waiting, hoping you'll call me,
I'm waiting, hoping I can have you.
I'm waiting, still waiting.
Do you love me?
I love you!

Natasha Graham (14)
St Monica's RC High School

My Family

My dad has hair as white as snow,
Some people call him Santa, you know.
But he isn't bad, he's my dad.

My mum is obsessed with cleaning,
She washes the windows until they are gleaming,
That's my mum, as happy as the sun.

My brother thinks he's really cool,
But really he's just a fool,
But I have to say sometimes he makes my day.

Finally my sister, she thinks she's the best,
But really she is a pest,
But overall, she's OK, so I hope you like my family.

Suzanne O'Donnell (11)
St Monica's RC High School

WE ALL FOLLOW UNITED

We flock beneath
The leaking corrugated roof
Wind howling
Rain dripping
Caught in the flickering headlights
Waiting patiently
The last remnants of a crowd.
The crowd comes alive
As the teams plod slowly
Kick about dispassionately
Waiting reluctantly
Whistles start to sound.
The game
Is like watching paint dry
With slow strides and no flow
Midweek
Mid-season
Mid-table
Nothing left to win or lose.
Nil-nil
To soft applause
Wet and wearily
The teams depart
Little boys chase their fallen idols
Across the muddy plain
And dream, one day
Of Premiership glory!

David Rogerson (15)
St Monica's RC High School

LOVE

Love is what it's all about,
It makes you want to scream and shout.
You find a partner,
You think they're great
You just hope they will be your mate.
You love them till the day they die,
You can't help it you just cry.

Laura Tierney (14)
St Monica's RC High School

LIFE

Life,
What an amazing thing,
Fragile, yet resilient,
Ugly, yet beautiful.

Life,
More precious than the largest diamond,
Yet treated as if it is little more than dust.

Carelessly,
Flames of life are snuffed out like a candle,
With no thought,
For its value.

Life,
A precious thing,
Never fully appreciated,
Until it's gone.

Daniel Minett (14)
St Monica's RC High School

AMOUR

Amour is love, but what happens to you?
Firstly butterflies fly around in your tummy
You cannot speak because you have a dummy
This is what love can do.

Amour is love, but what happens to you?
You feel light as the air and soon you can fly
But then you can't look them in the eye
This is what love can do.

Amour is love, but what happens to you?
You get goosebumps all over your skin
Admiring, you put your hands under your chin
This is what love can do.

Amour is love, but what happens to you?
The time is near, tell them how you feel
Now it's their heart for you to steal
This is what love can do.

Cesare Taurasi (14)
St Monica's RC High School

BONFIRE NIGHT

Bang, boom the fireworks go,
Flying and fizzling so high in the sky,
Colours so bright that they make your mind blow,
The sounds that they make fill your ears till they fry.
The sparklers' lights leap like frogs,
The sky is a sea of colour,
There is no space for miserable fog,
The treacle toffee makes you fuller and fuller,
Fireworks soar like a giddy little child,
Catherine wheels are all over,
Ecstatic little children are all going wild,
There is even a firework like a four-leaf clover.

Scott Gray (14)
St Monica's RC High School

SLAVERY

What is all this slavery about
Every day, week in, week out?
We're overworked and underfed,
We're tired of hearing the same thing said.
Whether the weather is hot or cold,
We've got to do what we are told.
Unless someone can see our plight,
It will spell the end for the Israelites.

God must have listened to our plea
Moses appeared to set us free
He tells the Pharaoh that he's not fair
To imprison his people within his lair.
If he doesn't set us free
We'll run away and divide the sea,
In a land of milk and honey
With valleys green and weather sunny.

Nicola Smith (13)
St Monica's RC High School

THIS WORLD IS NOT AT PEACE

This world is not at peace
Wars are going on
The sound of guns and bombs
Won't make the world go round.

This world is not at peace
There is a lot of evil
Cruel, greedy and selfish people
You can expect no mercy.

This world is not at peace
Fighting every day
Thousands of people fall
Only few survive.

This world is not at peace
But one day it will be
This time is not yet known
But hopefully soon to come.

Liam White (13)
St Monica's RC High School

LIFE

Life is a valuable thing
But we watch it fly by as the pendulum swings.
Our lives tick away every day
Eventually everything starts to decay.
Life doesn't last for ever
I don't know the answer why.
We'll never know the true answer
Even however hard we try.
Life is too short
It goes too fast
Everything will end
As nothing lasts.
Put simply it comes to this:
There's too much hate in this world
For life to exist.

Stephen Dooley (15)
St Monica's RC High School

THE DERBY

The teams ran out on the pitch
The crowd went wild for a while
And me a little speck
Standing in a sea of red.
Everyone smiled for a time
Until City put one in from the halfway line.

The first half was long
And City were very strong
But United had put two in the net
When the third crept in.

City battled but it was all in vain
As United led throughout the whole of the game
City knew it would end in pain.
City's confidence began to grow
Just as the final whistle was about to blow.

Howard Harrison (14)
St Monica's RC High School

MUSIC

My life would be meaningless without music
Never to hear a single song again,
Never to be able to dance and sing to it
It would be like forgetting how to hold my pen.

Pop, rock and R&B
These are the best types to me
Loads of bands that play their tunes
The DJs are scratching while the crowds go 'Boom'.
Backstreet Boys, O-Town and Blue are the best,
I think they're better than all the rest
When they're on stage Linkin Park and Limp Bizkit completely lose it
That is why my life would be meaningless without music!

Keely Grattidge (15)
St Monica's RC High School

WAR

The Grim Reaper stalks its prey,
Like a vulture waiting for its prey to die,
The stench of death fills the air.

Blood of comrades carpet the mud,
Guns go off with a terrible *thud!*
Bodies drooping all around.

Either side trying to even the score,
Half the world is at war.

How would you like to be sent away?
Away from your family, but for how long?
When will it be over?

You might think that it's cool, to go to war,
But if you really want to,
Then you're a terrible fool.

Fighting for your country,
Or so they say,
The memories you will have,
Will never go away.

Peter Riley (14)
St Monica's RC High School

FORMULA ONE

The crowds hustle and bustle as the countdown begins,
The cars take their places as the position bell rings.
Mechanics swarm around the cars, like bees to their hives,
They turn their spanners to fix the car into forward drive,
The car's bodywork gleams and glows,
But the question on the fans' minds is 'Who's going to win the show?'
The bees leave their hives as the final countdown is under way,
The clouds are clear, it's looking to be a fine day.
The countdown is over, the engines roar,
The rubber burning on the track floor.
As they race to the first corner for position on the track,
Two cars collide into the barriers, smack!
The pit stops are here, Schumacher's in first,
Oh no! His tyres just burst!
The end is here, who's going to win?
The answer is obvious, it's the flying Finn!

Mark Mottram (15)
St Monica's RC High School

THE CITY

This city howls with desolation
Empty buildings crumbling away
Narrow backstreets cold and deserted
Far from memories of glorious days.

Railroad tracks pulled up long ago
Last train came in sixty-two
Now the town is cold and empty
No one even passes through.

People upped and left this city
Down the highway they all drove
Looking for work across the border
Cooking on a camping stove.

Sleeping rough at the highway side
'Neath the burning of the stars
Bedding down in the soft sand
Or on the back seats of their cars.

Trying to settle in other towns
A whole new job, a whole new state
The old city still crumbles away
Deserted . . . abandoned . . . desolate.

Michael Grzesiak (15)
St Monica's RC High School

An English Summer's Day

I arose inside a sunbeam that morning,
The faint summer breeze danced merrily in the willows,
A sudden chill gave me a warning,
Yet the sun shone on as the day began.

As the clock chimed for seven,
A black cloud swallowed up the sky,
Like a devil shadowing over Heaven,
As angels watched below with fear.

But wait . . . in the distance I can see,
A ray of light in evil blackness.
The angels joined it, it seemed to me,
To overcome the misery and sadness.

The tiny ray grew into a sea of light.
The evil fled away.
For me this was a beautiful sight,
Now the door can open and the sun can shine on.

Mairéad Murphy (14)
St Monica's RC High School

Frrrizzled Like A *Frrritter!*

Down with children, one by one,
We will kill them just for fun.
We will squash them all till they're very small,
And turn them into things that crawl.
Witches rule because they're cruel.
Cruel and nasty is their rule.
Witches wear wigs that itch,
Every time they itch they do it with a twitch.
We will dress as women to disguise our looks,
No need to read those silly books.
Every day the witches cook,
Little boys, big boys caught by a hook,
We will destroy all the children no matter how they
Look!

Rebecca Harding (11)
St Monica's RC High School

NEW YORK NO MORE!

First it was the north tower, then it was the south,
Hijacked planes sliced the skycraping structures in half,
Filling the sky with huge grey clouds of dust.
Each tower collapsed without any warning with hundreds
of people trapped inside,
People jumping from windows and screaming for help,
Hoping someone could save them!
Rescue workers fled for their lives whilst others awaited their death!
No one could have imagined the devastation caused,
New York was in ruin with rubble and debris covering Manhattan,
And hundreds of families desperately searching for lost loved ones.
Lives have been shattered in every corner of the globe,
Whilst the hunt for remaining bodies amongst what used to
be the World Trade Center continues . . .

Katie-Louise Armitage (11)
St Monica's RC High School

CRUMBLED TO DUST

Misty ghosts of dust rose and meandered into the sorry sky.
The horrific scenes were shown on the news as I watched in terror . . .
Why?
Buildings which once stood proud and tall
Were shattered, scattered, crumbled to dust,
By heartless people hijacking a plane,
The Manhattan skyline would never be the same.
Panic-stricken, shocked and confused,
Ran the innocent victims,
Coated with an avalanche of the World Trade Center debris
Thousands killed and many more orphaned . . .
For that sad day September the eleventh, 2001 at eight forty-five,
Few people were lucky to survive,
And now we forever remember in our hearts,
The scenes of the buildings being shattered, scattered,
Crumbled to dust.

Charlotte Gray (11)
St Monica's RC High School

SEASIDE

The seaside is my favourite place
It has ice cream stalls that sell my favourite flavour, strawberry lace.
It is sometimes hot and sometimes windy
My little cousin sits on the sand with her Barbie and Sindy,
I build sandcastles tall and high
They are so high they can reach the sky,
I enjoy going in the sea
But last time I went in I was hit on my knee.
There are all sorts of creatures
And in the distance lots of other feathers,
But best of all the golden sands
When I pick it up, it rushes through my hands.

Nicola Struminskyj (12)
St Monica's RC High School

ANGELS

Their wings glisten as they fly so high,
All across the moonlit sky,
People sing and praise them all,
And hope that they will never fall.

God's messengers from up above,
Fly around like the bird of love,
Bringing happiness to one and all,
As they respond to every call.

Lyndsey Dockery (16)
St Monica's RC High School

GIRL

Are you standing upright,
And springing from your toes,
And walking tall and proud young girl,
So that everybody knows.

You are a wonder of the world, young girl,
You could make all eyes turn,
But you will learn all in good time,
The glances which do spurn.

Looks of admiration,
Stares you can't define,
Just take it in your stride, young girl.
And give them never mind.

As long as you are happy, confident and sure,
The world is set before you,
That and so much more.

Tara Gilbert (15)
St Monica's RC High School

AUTUMN

The autumn leaves are falling down,
The leaves are orange, yellow and brown.
The weather is sunny, bright and warm,
But it can thunder and blow up a storm.

The squirrels rush and hide in the trees,
But the leaves are gone, blown away in the breeze,
The farmers are busy collecting the hay,
The children won't help as they want to play.

The animals look hard for a place to sleep,
The forest is dark and gloomy but deep.
The trees look bare but the berries are red
Autumn is here but now it's time for bed.

Jack Makin (12)
St Monica's RC High School

THE CLEARING OF SOLITUDE

Deep into the dark forest,
Is a small clearing,
Which is lined with perfect trees
For hundreds of miles around.

The trees are dark, luscious and green,
And stand wearily upon the damp ground,
Their leaves and branches weave in and out,
Up and down, around and around.

The bright yellow sun slowly rises,
Peeping through the trees' tangled branches,
Gently warming the morning dew
Upon the forest floor.

The gentle meandering stream,
Slowly trickles down the rocky waterfall,
Weaving in and out of the trees'
Thick, large buttresses.

Oh, what an idyllic place!

Chris Travis (15)
St Monica's RC High School

PEACE AND VIOLENCE

People dead, what for?
The world is filled with all this violence.
Action is needed to stop this violence,
Care and consideration is what we need.
Endangered for ever.
Now I'm full of anger,
Others feel the same,
Then we go to war
What do we do
Armed with guns?
But riots never solve anything.

Pawlo Slawycz (14)
St Monica's RC High School

My Dear Wife

I have had a great loss in my life,
My loving, caring, dear, old wife;
She was just so beautiful, and so kind,
I don't think I could ever get her off my mind.

She had big, brown eyes, and long, dark hair
She used to cuddle me like a bear,
I wish she was still here living with me,
I would be so happy, full of glee.

I would do anything to get my sweetheart back,
The only person to comfort me is my best friend, Jack,
I should just forget about it, and I should not cry,
But I would rather it be me than her to die.

Jamie Lee (12)
St Monica's RC High School

PEACE, LOVE AND HARMONY

Peace, love and harmony
Is how the world should be,
A world full of happiness is,
A perfect world for me.

A world without fighting,
A world without war,
A world full of understanding
Is a world worth caring for.

Peace, love and harmony
Is a world that can be free
A world full of loving is a perfect
World to me.

Kayleigh Lord (13)
St Monica's RC High School

WAR AND PEACE

On the hills and mountains,
And along the seashore
Comes an old enemy, everlasting war
In the homes and gardens
The children play
In a tranquil world safe today.

For tomorrow the peace of the world,
Will crack in two
And hatred and suffering will pour right through
Yet the light of Heaven will show us the way
Soon hope, health and happiness will
Brighten our day.

Mark Wimbleton (12)
St Monica's RC High School

MY POEM

Sat on the sofa, telling endless stories,
She is like the wind,
Spontaneous and free-spirited,
Going where she wants to go,
Like the wind is sometimes light,
And sometimes strong
So is she,
Sometimes fun-loving, yet sometimes strict!
The best friend you never had,
The blue eyes truthful,
Her tanned skin ageing
And her blonde hair just hung there.
But when the wind has gone,
The leaves don't chase,
There is a stillness,
And the fun has gone.
Then when the wind returns,
The leaves start chasing.
Adventures return, stories continue,
The atmosphere is no longer tense.
Strong-headed, warmth and love,
Makes you feel special and wanted,
The child pours out of her.
She doesn't care what people think.
Yvonne Yanena Esmerelda Halska-Smith.
With a name like that you'd think she was royalty.
But it's just plain old Yvonne.
Yet, a queen in my eyes.
But one day the wind will have disappeared,
The stories will no longer be told
The fun, information, generosity,
Best friend and free spirit
Will die!

Katie Batterton (13)
St Monica's RC High School

My Grandad

My grandad, John, was number one
he'd four sons and two daughters.
One of them is my mum, the youngest is Stephen
he looks a bit like Tintin with his ginger hair.

My grandad was like the wind
he was always on the move
a bricklayer by day and an
entertainer by night.

He was married to my nana, Pat
who was always happy and never sad
until the wind went away.

When the wind went away
we were all very sad
because my grandad was
a wonderful man.

Anthony Birch (13)
St Monica's RC High School

PEACE

Peace is like a dove,
that flutters in the sky,
Peace is all around us,
like the night sky.
Love brings us beautiful things,
everyone is cuddled and curled,
that's what winter brings.
All around the world,
peace is hiding, maybe under a stone or a rose corner,
Everyone wants this devastation to end.
It's in everyone's heart, but politicians have to decide
where the troubles end.

Sarah Jones (15)
St Monica's RC High School

MY GRANDAD

Being a kind-hearted person,
my grandad invites me into his household,
being the loving person he is,
he asks me if I want a drink.
'Yes please,' I reply,
the frames of his glasses shimmer in the distance.

I put on the news to watch the latest news,
but I cannot let him hear it
or he will comment with not quite racist words.

But there is no chance of me missing him,
not because he is dead, because he is not,
but I don't believe I know anyone else
who can show so much love and kindness
towards his own grandson.

Liam Hodgetts (13)
St Monica's RC High School

My Best Friend Emma

Emma, my best friend
She is loyal and kind
And very hard to find.
She is always out cheering people up and
Putting great smiles on their faces.
Like Casper The Friendly Ghost does.

I always miss her when she's not there
But wherever she goes she will take good care.
She is well organised
Just like Casper.
She hates being told off
And doesn't do anything wrong.

Emma is funny, intelligent and bright
She would never get herself into a fight,
That's why I think my best friend Emma
Is just like Casper, The Friendly Ghost.

Simone Pendlebury (13)
St Monica's RC High School

THE CYCLE OF LIGHT

In from the sunshine, out of the light
Into the moonlight, that's when it's night
Continuous are the stars that shine
Up in the sky they look so fine.

The blanket of darkness which covers the sky
My head on the pillow as dreams pass me by
The dark passes on, as I sleep through the night,
I wake in the morning, when next comes the light.

The sun shines bright, surrounded by blue
It crosses the sky to warm me and you
Then once again the sun fades away
It all starts again, the very next day.

Annita Hearne (15)
St Monica's RC High School

A CHRISTMAS POEM

Beep, beep went the clock,
It was Christmas morning
When the sun was dawning,
I rushed over to check my Christmas sock . . .

I had everything I wanted but,
Had Santa really been?
My parents can't trick me; I'm not dumb,
But wait, something fell from the chimney covered in soot . . .

Who could that be I can only see his feet.
Yes, it's him 'Hello young fella, I've got to run,
I hope your presents will deliver fun!'
Seeing him has made my Christmas complete.

Luke Riley (14)
St Monica's RC High School

THE MARINER'S LIGHT

Far out to sea on a wild, stormy night,
There stood upon a rock, a bright light.
A powerful guardian, a ray of hope and life,
The star of the sea in peril and strife.

The saviour and warning to many a soul,
To the dangers lurking like a gaping hole.
To the ships it was a God of the glory
To sail away enlightened with their story.

To those whom the light saved
Eternally grateful for salvation from the grave.
To find the light was their endeavour
But far out to sea, it stands for ever and ever.

Richard Fenge (13)
St Monica's RC High School

I DON'T KNOW WHAT TO DO

I don't know what to do
For this poem I'm about to do
There are lots of things I could write about
I suppose I could do it about nowt.

It could be about football, music or anything
Maybe something that I find interesting.
Either way, I just don't know what to do
For this poem I've got to do.

I could write a poem about music
I play a guitar, it's electric,
In a band that plays a fast tempo.
Oh, I still don't know what to do.

If it was about something interesting,
I could do it about motor racing.
Schumacher, Coulthard and Irvine too
I suppose this will just have to do.

David Corkill (15)
St Monica's RC High School

THE MUM I KNOW

From the bed she rose as a pillow,
Her gentle heart starting a new day,
Small and soft to show affection
Her warm voice easing my morning.

Light and cuddly to greet me
When I open my wary eyes,
She smells clean and cleansed
As she does everyday.

Her smooth coat of fleecy wool,
Making me feel cosy and happy.
Reassuring me and encouraging me
She is perfect to have and to hold.

Izabel Burton (14)
St Monica's RC High School

MY DAD

When I see my dad I am happy.
He is just like a bear,
When he gives me a hug, he squeezes me and he's cuddly and warm.

Every time I see him he looks and gets older every day.
He gets softer and taller.

He is noisy.
He moans and groans, he sulks nearly all day.
He is very moody and sensitive and gets hungry.

He is sleepy and he sleeps a lot of the day.
He works hard and scares me when he yawns.

He is very brave, he goes to different places
With different people every day.

He is my dad.
He is just like a bear,
He encourages me and supports me through those rotten days.
He may shout and moan at me, but when he's not there,
There's a piece of me that isn't.
I only see him a few times, so when I see him
I make the best of it.

Gareth Winney (14)
St Monica's RC High School

MY DAD

I walked in to see him sprawled across the couch
like the roots of a tree.
He looked up with his stubbly face and at first scared me
but then I realised that it was only him.

The couch is big, but my dad is bigger because his feet
were hanging off the edge looking all straggly
and waving about like the waves in the sea,
with no definite shape.

He had blue slippers on which were old and worn away
and had small pieces of thread hanging off.
He had a camouflaged jacket which was like a forest,
a green T-shirt which was the colour of fields,
and some jeans which were worn at the knees
and the colour of a lake from the distance.

Danny Coughlin (14)
St Monica's RC High School

LIFE AND DEATH

Life is defined as a journey
Which takes you from cradle to grave
It can pass you by before you know it
So every precious moment, you should save

Everyone hopes for a good, long life
To get what they want from this life
But death's always around the next corner
And the journey can be filled with strife

No one can define what a precious moment is
It changes from person to person
Bungee jumping and such thrills are for some
Or the ordinary things like the rising of the sun

So don't let your life pass you by
Treasure the little things too
Everyone plans for their future
But the end can come out of the blue.

Matthew Barton (15)
St Monica's RC High School

TOO MANY CHOCOLATES

You don't scare me. I scare myself.
You may hurt me with your spoken words
but I have heard worse and I am strong.
You may touch me, I won't feel you.
You may look into my eyes with care
but I will look upon someone else.
You won't influence me. I am not naive.
You may wish to mould me like you have before,
but I've dug out my old favourite jeans.
You may laugh at me, I see the joke.
You may try and tempt me as I've been tempted before,
but one too many chocolates can make you ill.

Mark Abbott (15)
St Monica's RC High School

MORNING GLORY

A chink of light
The song of the lark
I hear distant bells
Calling out in the dark.

The slow rhythm of breathing
A beat of the heart
The dawn of the morning
I wake with a start.

The bells are still ringing
My ears are in shock
My eyes are still searching
As I reached for the clock.

Harry Green (11)
St Monica's RC High School

My Love For This Woman

My love for this woman is so great,
Being born unto her is much more than just fate.
Though once a woman of vast men and power
Is now just a sapling or a weed or a flower.

This lady made up of red, white and blue,
Gave security to folks like me and you.
No longer a force, grand with Empire,
But has quietened down like that of a fire.

So her days some say, may be numbered now,
Split up into two, farewell, ciao!
Unknown what is to be of the unconquerable people
Ad jur Madame, though all hope is not feeble.

I hope the fair maiden's future's not Euro,
But I will always love her dear though,
For she founded this world with you and I,
So I hope she will never die.

Joseph Mycock (14)
St Monica's RC High School

THE BATTLE

Sling stones rattled against the battlements like hail on a tin roof,
Arrows buzzed like angry wasps,
On the ground woodlanders fought vermin, paw to paw,
War cries ripping from their throats.
Steel clashed against steel as rapiers and scimitars crossed.
In the middle of the melee was an immense male badger
With bloodlust in his eyes.
He struck left and right with his great halberd,
Cutting down sea rogues.
Upon the battlements a garrulous hare was shouting
'Come on chaps, wot wot, show those vermin chappies
What a battle really is!'
Then came a cry above the melee, 'Back to the ship me hearties!'
At this, the vermin fled.
A great cheer ripped from the throats of the woodlanders,
They had won!

Claire Boucher (14)
St Monica's RC High School

How Cold Is The Heart?

How cold is the heart?
Is it cold enough to hit and beat a child
Till they cry and their heart turns as cold as yours?
All it ever wanted was love, laughter
And happiness in their life.

How cold is your heart?
Cold enough to love someone
Like they were your own
Flesh and blood, then to turn
Your back on them like they were
Nothing?

How cold is the heart?
Enough to fall out with a best friend
Then to hear that they died
Never getting to say sorry
Is your heart as cold as that?

Ciara Boardman (10)
St Monica's RC High School

TERROR IN AMERICA

Death and destruction,
The mess of an eruption.
Two towers
Just hours from
Death and destruction,
Once standing proud
Now laying on the ground.
Exploded
Like fireworks of debris
A desperate search
Through the murk
The sight of death and destruction.

The place that was once alive
Has taken a great nosedive
Depression!
Survivors remember the 11th of September
But mourn.
A great sorrow we look to tomorrow,
With hope
Silence.
The sound of death and destruction.

Jennifer Raggett (15)
St Monica's RC High School

ANIMALS IN DANGER

Going for five pounds
A gorilla's hand as an ashtray.
The sound of a whale going over the scale,
The sound of a shark, like a bark.
The sound of a vulture hovering over its prey,
The elephant trumpets to keep the tiger at bay.
The hunter becomes the hunted as animals
Fight back to survive.

Coleen Quinn (14)
St Monica's RC High School

STRONGER

Look down and see skin shining, black and blue
Blood of the innocent is seeping through
A barking is pounding through her head
Each night she crouches below her tiny bed.

Loving and caring for her, left behind
Dreams of a loving family are in her mind
Whilst trapped in a chamber of pots and pans
Surrounded by fear whilst she rubs her hands.

Now she is far away and with her no longer
Away from the pain and she has grown stronger
Now she looks back and she feels full of anger
Through her mind and her bones and through each finger.

She feels no pity nor sorrow for her
But all she will say is 'God bless her'
Never can she call or address her as Mother
But she thanks her
For helping her to this point, like no other.

Regina Cheng (15)
St Monica's RC High School

Rushing From The Mills - 1930

People rushing back and forth
Coming from the mills
So they can pay their bills
In the high green hills.

People slouched on the ground
After a hard day at work,
But when the people go from work you
Will see the boss lurk.

Every night he walks back and forth,
Checking all of the rooms
And the rusty looms.

Horse-drawn carriages racing round,
And it makes a lot of galloping sounds
Like a mad rock band.

Daniel Fowler (12)
St Monica's RC High School

LOVE = HATE

The world is inside out
Hell is on the outside
How does hate begin?
Probably by love!

Love of their religion
Love of their country
But is it true love?
When hate leads the way!

People fight
Their rage ignites
For what?
Their so-called beliefs!

These people know peace is right
And still they continue to cause pain.
What is it that makes them so?
Their pride stands too high!

Andrei Michaluk (16)
St Monica's RC High School

MY DOG

I have a funny dog
Who's as funny as she can be.
But everywhere I want to go, she always follows me.
When it's dinner time she comes and sits near me
For I always take her for a walk
After she's finished her tea.

At night-time she waits
Until I come to bed
And then when she jumps up to join me
She snuggles against my head.

Sometimes at night she gets cold
So she climbs up my sheet
Until she finds a perfect spot that's right
In between my feet.

She wakes me up each morning
By jumping on my belly
So we both get up and race downstairs
So we can watch some telly.

Mark Barlow (13)
St Monica's RC High School

MY GRANDFATHER

Waking up from his deep sleep in hospital,
His feet curled up because the bed is too small,
He lies there with pipes everywhere,
Then tells us he will never leave us.

It's sad to think he's on his own
Just looking at four walls
It's sad to see him as he is
Hooked up here and there.

I cried, I cried. Oh how I cried!
My Grandad might be dying.

His body is crooked, like a winding path
I love him so very dearly
He's back to sleep
In a very deep sleep.

The next stage is a tracheotomy.

Rebecca Bowring (14)
St Monica's RC High School

GRANDMA'S LIKE A TAPESTRY

My grandma's like a tapestry
Needles weaved into her jumper
Seated by the glowing fire
Old threads clinging to her static jumper.

My grandma's warm and cuddly like a patchwork quilt,
Peering into the photo albums.
Memories stuck into each page.
My grandma's like a tapestry.

Strands of silver hair sparkle like a spider's web
Eyebrows like a feather stitch,
Lips stained like raspberry wool,
My grandma's like a tapestry.

Alice Babb (13)
St Monica's RC High School

PERFECT PLANET

Oh how I would love the world to be,
A safe, peaceful haven for you and for me.
No war or conflict between the races,
No terrorist attacks on any places.

A variety of life lived in harmony,
Free from ill-feeling, a heavenly place to be.
A tolerant society I'm certain would be best,
Less hatred and evil to put us to the test.

Love, warmth and affection would shine from us all,
Happy, smiling faces, proud people walking tall.
Chasing rainbows, walking free, enjoying a simple pleasure,
Living life to the full, collecting moments to treasure.

Going out, having fun, supporting one another,
Showing kindness and a helping hand to each and every brother.
Family life lived in a tranquil setting,
Loving God and each other, forgiving and forgetting.

Lauren Doyle (14)
St Monica's RC High School

My Best Friend

Sleeping, sleeping and sleeping
She lies there sprawled strangely on the bed
Warm and cosy, her light all sparked out
Her head in its usual land of dreams.

When finally up and awake
Her light now back on again,
She's bright and full of life
And smiling her beautiful smile.

Her big bold eyes alight like two bulbs
Her rosy red cheeks glowing with love
Her warmth shining like the rays of a light,
And her generosity and kindness standing out.

She's friendly to everyone and doesn't stop chatting,
And her helpful advice always helps to guide my path.
She stands out with her lit-up blonde hair,
And grabs the room with a high pitched laugh.

Like a light she makes the dark moments seem bright
She makes me laugh with stories and jokes,
She's fun and energetic
But usually just wants to stay in bed.

Her loving tenderness goes on and on
And her blinding light constantly shines through
Right until darkness returns when she's
Sleeping, sleeping and sleeping.

Charlotte Forshaw (13)
St Monica's RC High School

POP STARS

Pop stars are everywhere you go
You see them on the TV and listen to them on the radio.
Singing and dancing is what they like to do
Their job is to entertain you.

The girls like the boy bands; Five, Westlife and O-Town
The boys like the girl bands; Atomic Kitten, Super
Sister and Destiny's Child.

You go to a concert to watch them do their stuff
But when you leave you don't think it's enough.

Katie Stewart (13)
St Monica's RC High School

THE NIGHTMARE?

Aaagh!
My eyes went snap,
the fear showing in the dilated pupils.
My breath coming out in short, sharp gasps,
as if there were only thick smog to inhale.

I looked around me at the
patterns of the shadows making dark,
deadly pictures like disfigured monsters,
mirroring the ones of my nightmare.

As my eyes passed over these
distorted pictures,
my heartbeat sounded as if it was
the drum of war.
Thumping the advance of the two armies.

I turned my head quickly, trying to find peace.

Next to me was my little sister,
quietly murmuring the song of sleep.
Her face was full of innocence like
a white lamb not yet seeing
the world of hatred.

Her delicate curls fell around her head
as if they had been arranged by
some unearthly creature.

By looking at this angel

I soon forgot hatred in
the pictures of my dream

The hatred

Of the world.

Anna Purdue (14)
St Monica's RC High School

THE MYSTERY CAT

His mischief goes around,
You pass him and you make no sound.
Sometimes you say,
That he has his own way.

Then you see
That he can be
A trespasser to your street,
Sound comes back, like you're in for a treat.

When you cross eye to eye,
You never know when you will die.
He comes to you,
From out of the blue.

Delphine Littler (12)
St Monica's RC High School

TIME

I sit and wonder how time goes by.
I think where I will stand in the vastness of time.
Will I be remembered in years to come?
How will I be remembered when seas that have engulfed lands
have dried and died and grains of sand have formed to take their place?

We are but grains of sand in the complexity of time.
Imagine all the people who have wandered on the Earth,
Breathed the sweetness of the air and moved and lived in the stillness
of time.
But when I am gone and the Earth has withered and died
Will time have existed
Or was it just invented by clever men?

Paul Knowles
St Monica's RC High School

Water And Nature

Water brings life,
Water brings death,
Fun and games,
Splashing fun,
Burning boats,
Viking burials.

Drinking, washing,
Cooking, cleaning,
Drowning, fearing,
Ashes scattered on a turbulent sea.

Nature is a miracle,
Full of life and death,
Never starting,
Never stopping,
It has always been.

Nature is made of miracles,
Miracles are nature,
Not just the world,
Not just the galaxy,
Not just the universe,
But beyond,
Always it will rein,
And so be it.

Siobhan Wilkinson (14)
St Monica's RC High School

JAMIE

As he sits there playing on his games console,
He doesn't think of the pain or the hole
That he has left in this family's life.
The hurt still stabs them like a knife,
Soon he will be out; he doesn't care
This isn't justice, this isn't fair.
It has only been eight years
Since he caused all those tears.
He cut school with his mate
And led a young boy to his fate.
They took him to a train track, poured paint into his eyes,
Then they kicked him to try and stop his cries.
Finally his screams could be heard no more,
He just lay there on the floor.

What were their thoughts? They were only ten years old,
How could their hearts have been so bitter and cold?
For the past eight years they have been locked away
And not been allowed to see reality or the true light of day.
But soon they'll have to survive on their own,
They'll each be given a new identity and a new home.
Everyone knows this isn't fair,
It's Jamie Bulger's family's worst nightmare.

Every person in the country will try and track them down,
They will be hunted for and thrown out of every town.
At worst they might be killed
And then that hole in this family's life might be filled.
But that's not what they want; they just want to get on with life,
And end all this hatred, suffering and strife.
They know the memories they have of Jamie are the best,
They just want to finally lay him down to rest.

Stephanie Burke (15)
The Swinton High School

JUST ANOTHER ORDINARY DAY

It's just another ordinary day
The paperwork is piled everywhere
And the phone is ringing non-stop
Looks like there isn't going to be one minute spare.

I've only been in the office for five minutes
And already it's extremely busy in here
But that's usual for this workplace
And I must admit, I like the atmosphere.

I have my young children to support
Although I hate to leave them with the sitter
My job is an outlet from all the chaos
Which, if I stayed with, would turn my love bitter.

Well! I'd better get back to my work now.
I need to ring London . . . Whoa! What's that?
Everything is shaking, people are screaming,
Something must be happening . . . but what?

I must see what's going on, I must get out
But the doorway's filled with flames; I'm trapped in here
I need to escape; I have a family to love.
I'm going to die, my body's trembling with fear.

What shall I do with my last few moments on Earth?
I have to ring my family, but what shall I say?
The answer machine has come on, how do I explain?
Well here goes 'To my babies, I love you more with every day.'

Tears are filling my eyes, I can barely speak,
I'm never again going to see the sun set over the sea
Or hear birds sing on a new summer's day.
It's the end; the walls are collapsing all around me.

The World Trade Towers are giving way
On this, just another ordinary day.

Hollie Cheadle (15)
The Swinton High School

AMERICA - YOU ARE NOT ALONE

You are not alone
We share your hurt and sorrow
We feel your heartache and your pain
As you cry into tomorrow
So many innocent lives lost
Such sadness has gripped the nation
A fearful terrorism act
Which caused so much devastation
To think of what they went through
That horror-stricken day
Brings tears to the eyes of every person
Feelings, words cannot say
We wish our arms could embrace you
As you shed your never-ending tears
If we stand side by side, we'll get through it
We will cast aside our own fears
Those who died will rest in peace
They will always be in our thoughts
Their memories will forever live on
But for now we offer our support
Never give up, try and be strong
Even though you feel you can't cope
Whoever did this will pay severely
Just remember never give up hope
And for those who showed so much courage
By saving lives and losing their own
We praise you from the bottom of our hearts
You are not alone.

Simona Gargiulo (15)
The Swinton High School

ROCK GIFT

A knock at your door
Pierces the silent air
And awakens you from slumber.
As you stagger downstairs
You can barely see the darkened figure,
Through the translucent glass of your door
It seems scared, as it scurries
Down you garden path
You slowly open the door
To find a small box on your doorstep
You're reluctant to pick it up
You're afraid, but also curious
As to what lies in the box
Eventually you carefully carry it
Into your bedroom, your home.
You slowly unwrap the box . . .
Its plain, dusty, copper-like paper
To reveal a plain grey rock
Carefully wrapped in pink tissue paper
Like a sleeping baby in a blanket.
The rock had a rough surface, but,
You look through the ugliness and find a beauty.
You pretend to throw it away
But you secretly keep it . . .
. . . in the back of your wardrobe
. . . in the back of your mind.

Hannah Jackson (15)
The Swinton High School

MY BABY

She won't shut up, she just keeps screaming.
She never stops crying, her eyes are streaming.
I've tried her bottle, she just spat it out.
She isn't hungry, there isn't a doubt.
I keep changing her nappy,
It's not making her happy.
She's tried playing with toys,
But she won't stop the noise.
She carried on all through the night,
I have to get her out of my sight,
I can't escape the crying,
I've given up trying.
I clutch my pillow and run to the cot,
I hold it to her face, I can't make myself stop.
She whimpers and stops crying for once,
I try shaking her but there is no response.
Her body is limp; I can't shake these fears,
Why isn't she breathing? I now long for her tears.
She was tiny and helpless, I realise it now,
I loved her so much and I ask myself how.
She only wanted to be held and cradled to sleep,
Now she's sleeping forever, never again will she weep.
She was my only child; I can't believe what I've done,
I should never have been able to become a mum.

Claire Dempsey (15)
The Swinton High School

MY BENGAL EAGLE OWL

She opens her wings
Spreading them wider
As she takes off
I wait in the garden
Suddenly, she returns
Swooping, swiftly from the sky
She lands on my glove.
Then and only then
Does she comb
Through her feathers
With her sharply curved beak
Unruffled by her adventures.

Nick Hartley (15)
Trinity CE High School

WOMAN OF THE FUTURE

I am a child
I am all the things of my past:
My mother's hair, thick and dark,
My father's eyes, dark and serious.
I am all I see:
Wars and violence on the television,
The soft sand on the beach.
Cute animals, begging to be stroked.
I am all I hear:
'Look after you brothers whilst I'm out.'
'Is he your boyfriend?'
Waves lapping at the beach . . .
The soft call of the birds in the morning.
I am all I feel:
The smooth skin of my friend's python
As I held it in my hands.
The soft hairy back of a tarantula.
I am all I remember:
My old life in Weston-Super-Mare,
My friends still living there.
My best friend dying a few weeks ago.
I am all I've been taught:
How to read, write and spell.
I am all I think:
Secrets, deep down inside
Never been revealed.
And one day I will grow and change
Like a chick
Breaking out of its shell
Beginning a new life
Because
I am a woman of the future.

Naseem McDermaid (13)
Trinity CE High School

I HAVE LIVED A THOUSAND YEARS

In suffocating cattle cars
Away from our homes, we were taken far.
The people shed bitter tears,
I have lived a thousand years.

We worked and died
However hard we tried,
Whilst the Germans laughed, talked and drank beer
I have lived a thousand years.

Bodies scattered in the square,
Cloth woven from human hair.
An SS guard stands and leers,
I have lived a thousand years.

Many Jews do not survive,
Whilst others seem barely alive,
Their families were gassed, screaming with fear.
I have lived a thousand years.

I have lived a thousand years,
Herded about like a frightened deer.
I'm a shadow of the past; my former life
Has vanished in a trice.

I have lived a thousand years and
experienced the Holocaust.

Louise Rashman (13)
Trinity CE High School

READING

Reading is getting lost in a book,
Reading is another world where you can
go in and out when you like.
Reading is a friend you can go to,
Reading is exciting and adventurous
or it could be dangerous and scary.
Reading is being able to understand
other people's life situations.
Reading is educational, it teaches you about
experiences you might have whilst growing up.
Reading is one of the best things invented by mankind.
Reading is my favourite hobby.

Carrie Thompson (13)
Trinity CE High School

WHAT IS SPRING?

So what really is spring?
Is it when little baby buds appear on the trees?
Or is when the days just get longer and longer?
Or is it when Dad brings the clock forward?
Or is it when the leaves come back on the trees?
Or is it when the sun comes out?
Spring, is all of these things.

Joanna Douglas (13)
Trinity CE High School

SELF-DEFENCE GRADING

I sat there on the bench
Waiting in turn,
Will I break it, will my hand start to burn?
What if I forget my movements?
I observe all the other students.
Then it's me next!
Will I pass the test?
'Long fist,' yells the teacher.
This is going to take too long.
I stop, suddenly I start to remember every part
The punching, the kicking,
The shouting, the hitting.
Now the final test.
I say to myself,
Do your best.
I stare at the tiles
Four are in front of me.
How I will break them, I don't really see.
I take a deep breath,
Then let it all out
Smash the tiles with an almighty shout.
I look down at the rubble on the floor.
I don't have to worry anymore,
Now I've got my next belt,
And no one will ever know
Just how proud I felt!

Cassie Brown (14)
Trinity CE High School

PICTURE THIS SILENCE

Picture this silence,
A shining white glimmer of trees and grass.
No footprints in the snow,
No birds singing in the trees.
The wind blowing through the snow-covered branches
Picture this silence.

Susannah Young (12)
Trinity CE High School

THE ROYAL EXCHANGE

Before the play
Sitting (or standing)
Talking with friends.
When the people with the bell come round
Dingalingalingalinga . . .
There is a mad rush for the doors.
Usherettes checking tickets,
People going in the wrong doors
Coming out again,
Dashing before the play starts
To buy last minute chocolates,
Sinking thankfully into their seats.
Then . . .
The lights go down
There is a *sshh*uration
Of people telling other people to 'Sshh!'
And generally making more noise
Than the people talking in the first place!
Then . . .
There's a blast of music
Or thunder
Or a voice
To make everyone jump,
The play has begun.
The audience leans forward in anticipation,
How will the plot unfold?

Ellie Bryce (13)
Trinity CE High School

SACRIFICE

Everyone is shouting and screaming,
Men, women, children and friends.
As first one plane crashes into a high building,
Then another and another.
Tears of sadness fill everyone's eyes
As we hear the screams of horror.
Only a few could escape.
Loves ones, lost because of the terrible disaster.
It makes me want to cry.

Ruth Paul (12)
Trinity CE High School

AMERICA

A ll those people killed
M en, women, children, gone forever
E veryone is terrified
R evolted, shocked
I magination reels, awareness of war!
C rying people in the street
A wareness of war

Jacob Robert Mason (11)
Trinity CE High School

FIRST DAY

My brain was all over the place like an aeroplane flying
My body was shrinking
I felt as if I had to go to outer space
I sweated and nervously nibbled my nails,
My heart was like a big bass drum saying 'Help!' and 'Stop!'
I worried that I might have no friends
My imagination spoke to me in miserable moans,
I checked to find my school clothes ready,
My mouth as dry as the air.
I thought I'd look silly in my uniform
My head was spinning round and round
My brain reeling
My heart pumping
My pulse racing
Would older ones push and shove us, stamp on us even?
Would the teachers be strict?
Would I fit in my new school?

Zachary Osawe (11)
Trinity CE High School

SHADOWS OF THE FLAME

The fire begins
Just a stroke of a match
Illuminating the wall
Casting shadows.

Shadows that flicker
Never stay focused,
Fidgeting, fussing,
Almost like dancing.

Shaking about, twirling
Hurling itself into a
Luminous dance.
Prancing and waving.

Full body movements
Hips swinging to the
Crackling fire's beat
Fire vibes in motion

Then slowly, surely
The fire dies down
No more energetic fire flames
In a final puff of smoke, it dies down.

Chikayla Coleman (13)
Trinity CE High School

SACRIFICE

Through these tiring, terrifying days of suffering,
Sacrifices have been made.
One man called his wife and said
'Hon I'll give it a go.'
He shocked his wife - gave up his life - for others
A sacrifice . . .
This is a sacrifice.
The terrorists too
Sacrificed their lives to avenge
What they thought was wrong.
Through balls of fire and billowing smoke,
Firemen went to save lives
When the World Trade Towers crashed!
They knew the dangers,
Yet they never lingered . . .
What a sacrifice.

Amanda D D Haynes (11)
Trinity CE High School

THE VALUE OF PEOPLE

P eople are priceless and irreplaceable
E ach one different in his own way
O ne person makes a difference to so many others
P arents, relatives, friends and children,
                    so that when that one person is
L ost
E veryone is affected.

If the loss of one person can cause so much sadness,
imagine the sadness caused by the loss of thousands.

Aimée Basson (11)
Trinity CE High School

A NEW WORLD?

D oes this mean a new world?
E ven now it shocks me.
V irtually death in the skies
A ny survivors are very lucky.
S uicide bombers, hijacked planes
T owers, lives and dreams, all gone.
A ll it equals is death and destruction.
T he destruction has left us all devastated.
I nternational mayhem.
O n the 11th of September 2001
N ever again do I want to see this cruelty.

Steven Sandbach (11)
Trinity CE High School

I WISH

I wish I could . . .
Travel the world on an aeroplane,
Go to Germany, Paris or Spain.

Pass my GCSEs
Finish school
Have my own mansion and swimming pool.

Live in New York
Shop every day,
Do what I want to
And have my own say.

I wish I could do all of these things,
I wish,
I wish,
I wish . . .

Hibo Arteh (12)
Trinity CE High School

HOCKEY

I love hockey
I've played for Manchester.
Usually I play right back,
Sometimes I play midfield
I love
Dribbling
Running
Defending
Attacking
Tackling
And *shooting!*
It is a hard sport
Because we are always
Running non-stop,
Till we are out of breath!
Hockey players
Must be fit and strong,
Play hard and never give in.

Anthony Brennan (14)
Trinity CE High School

PHOTOS SAY IT ALL

Photos say it all.
How tasteless your parents were
in dressing you when you were little.
The way the school photographer said
'Smile!' in that annoying tone.
The way you want to scowl, but have to look
nice in front of the camera.
Photos say it all.
The way people pose in that model wannabe way.
How much fun you had on that holiday in Spain.
How much you've changed.
Photos say it all.
How unhappy she looked when you took a photo
of her when she wasn't watching.
How sweet you looked, playing with your sisters
in the park and how much you have grown
to hate them!
How nice your older sister looked, kitted out in
your summer dress, sandals, summer hat,
eyeshadow, lipstick . . . and wait!
Are those your knickers you can see under
your dress?
They are . . .
Lauren get down here! Who said you could
wear my knickers?
They were the expensive ones that mum bought me.

Grace Dobson-Hughes (12)
Trinity CE High School

AMERICA'S DISASTER

America's disaster shook the world
The tragedy paralysed the Earth.
Everyone froze
In horror, shock and confusion.
The death of one affects many.
The world offers its sympathy,
But will it satisfy
The angered and disturbed souls of America?
This is a disgrace to the human race!

Jamie Holmes-Valentine (12)
Trinity CE High School

SEPTEMBER THE ELEVENTH

My mind is full of tragedy,
Why?
Why did the pilot do it?
The big tower is on fire
We can see a plane sticking out!
Then crash, the first tower crumples.
Topples down.
One, two, three seconds later,
The second comes down.
Everyone . . . workers, family and friends are
Trapped underneath.
Please help the people trapped under that rubble.

Chantel Cupitt (12)
Trinity CE High School

EGG

Inside
A twinkling shell
Lies a sleeping power
As it sleeps its tiny body forms.
Sitting in a home of moss and twigs
A little treasure held within a world of white,
At last the shell can hold no longer
It splits and cracks
And from the shell emerges
A jewel of nature
It awakens and emits a cry that makes the Earth smile.
Finally the wait is over
He feels the life surge through him.

Alex Hatton (12)
Trinity CE High School

HOME SWEET HOME

Home, home wonderful home, it's straight after school!
You jump into bed and blast music out loud,
You forget about school and relax, relax!

Wake up in the morning, lying in bed,
Your mum shouts 'Come for breakfast!'
You fill your bag up with books, and off to school we go,
Orrr!

Elliot Farrell (11)
Wright Robinson Sports College

THE LAST FEW DAYS OF PRIMARY SCHOOL

The last few days of primary school,
Easy days learning a song for assembly
Friends going to different schools
Laughter turns to tears
Tears to goodbyes
Hugging
Swapping phone numbers
First few days of high school homework
One teacher turns to six
Bus rides
Season change.

I'm in the big school now!

Holly Shelmerdine (11)
Wright Robinson Sports College